She-The Light of My Life

AF624673

OrangeBooks Publication

1st Floor, Rajhans Arcade, Mall Road, Kohka, Bhilai, Chhattisgarh 490020

Website: **www.orangebooks.in**

© Copyright, 2025, Author

All rights reserved. No part of this book may be reproduced, stored in a retrieval system, or transmitted, in any form by any means, electronic, mechanical, magnetic, optical, chemical, manual, photocopying, recording or otherwise, without the prior written consent of its writer.

First Edition, 2025

ISBN: 978-93-6554-649-1

Price: Rs. 299.00

The opinions/ contents expressed in this book are solely of the author and do not represent the opinions/ standings/ thoughts of OrangeBooks.

Printed in India

She

THE LIGHT OF MY LIFE

"A Collection Of Love And Grace For The One Who Redefined My World"

ANITHA MGM

OrangeBooks Publication
www.orangebooks.in

To God, With All My Heart

Before the first word was written, before the first memory found its way into verse —

You were there, shaping the silence into strength and the pain into purpose.

Every line of this book, every whisper of love, reflects Your grace.

"This was the Lord's doing;
It is marvellous in our eyes."

— Psalm 118:23

"The Lord directs the steps of the godly. He delights in every detail of their lives. Though they stumble, they will never fall, for the Lord holds them by the hand."

— Psalm 37:23–24

For the gift of *her*,

For the gift of love that heals,

For the gift of purpose that uplifts —

Thank You, Lord.

With boundless gratitude.

Dedication

To the Woman Whose Smile Became My Reason to Write...

Dear Geetha Miss…

This book is not just a collection of poems—It's a collection of everything I ever felt when You entered my world.

You taught me more than subjects—

You taught me to feel, to observe, to admire, and above all... to write.

This is for You.

Only for You.

Always about You…

Content

O Lord, Tell Her Everything

O Lord! Tell her everything—
How deeply I Love her, from the very core of my Heart!
When she stepped into my heart and made he
dwelling,
I offered my Soul,
To grace her with the purest gift I could give.
She showed me how to Love—
And in her light, my soul became whole, became pure.
Her Eyes, like Fire—burning when I dared to gaze,
Yet her Voice, like Snow—soothing, calm, and healing.
Perhaps, she shares a bond with the Moon,
For her face seems carved straight from the Heavens!
No word could ever define her nature—

So rare, so Unique—

And that, too, is why I Love her so.

O Lord! Tell her everything,

She is not only my Teacher—

But truly… my Everything.

On a Fine Teacher's Day

Under the trees she stood
In attire pink,
Within a wink,
She made my heart sink;
I stared at her with no blink:

Today my heart's grandee,
Looked like a cotton candy,
The eyes of mine turned unhandy.
The way she smiled
Tickled my heart,
And made me create on her an art;
Infinite are the memories
She poured in my mind pot.

She walked with a walk

That could even make the French rose talk;

She turned around with a spark,

Showered the words

Of honey from her stock.

I just love the way she is,

The only reason for my inner peace...!

Some Days, All

There are some days, when I miss her
And yearn to see her smile.
There are some days, I roam around
Like a mad.
Some days I wish to be her stamping sand,
Some days I want to be a flower on her band,
Some days I long to be the land she stands.
Some days I starve to hear the words she speaks,
Some days I adore the way she freaks.
Some days I dream her face in sleep,
Some days I see her world so deep.
Some days I like to be her shadow,
Some days my heart feels so low.
Some days I try to tell her what I feel,
Some days I have her thoughts as my meal.

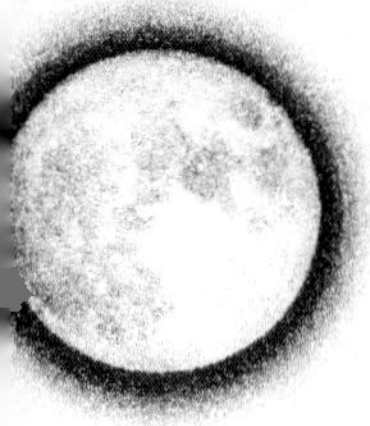

Some days I desire to be the one she likes,

With her presence, my heart gets hike.

Some days I strive for the care she shows,

Each day, my love for her never fails to grow...!

When the Sky Fell for Her

The Moon shines so bright from miles,
And admires the way she smiles.
The gentle wind blows out and sings,
She is an Angel with no wings.
The stars peek out just to see,
The grace she holds so effortlessly.

She, the One Beyond Compare

The beauty of her smile
Ceased my heart for a while;
The sweetness of her speech
Made me to reach
The highest place without any wings.
She is completely a miracle,
That wanders with a crackle;
Showers happiness everywhere
With her each stare.
She is the one who is symbol of care,
It's the reason why she has no compare...!

The One Who Lights the lives

The bright Sun,
And the shining Moon,
Makes me wonder that she is their teacher,
Because only she knows the magic
How to light her students' lives...!
With a smile so calm, and a soul so wise,
She turns the dullest days into sunrise.

The One My Heart Longs to Tell

I wish I could tell her everything
That my heart feels;
With her smile, my words she steals.
Like a watered flower, her voice falls,
To listen more, my heart scrolls.
She has such beauty,
Even the flowers could be jealous of.
A glance at her gesture stuns the mind,
And all my thoughts bind.
Her silence speaks more than words,
My heart flutters like a bird.
She is the one to be adored,
Who gives eternal memories in life to be stored...!

More Than a Flower

She is not just a flower to be smelt and left,

But a flowering tree that brings happiness with its each blossom,

Which is to be adored forever and ever...

Her presence paints peace on passing days,

Like a soft breeze that in silence sways,

She blooms in hearts in countless ways.

Her Smile, My Guiding Light

When I feel like everything in my life goes wrong,
Her divinely smile is the only reason,
That sets me to the path of flawlessness.
Her voice—like dawn—clears my darkness,
Her gaze brings hope, calm and brightness,
She is the reason behind my silent boldness.

A Moment That Stays Forever

Finally, I got to meet her—

And with just a smile,

She made me forget all my piled-up troubles...

A small walk beside her,

Just to make that moment worth remembering;

In just a few seconds,

She gave me a lifetime of thoughts to rewind.

I had planned to pour out

Everything my heart's been carrying...

But before I could,

Time tapped me on the shoulder,

Telling me it was time to say goodbye...

Still, that one moment—

Is enough to carry me through the coming days...!

Anitha Mgm

The Epic She Unfolded in Me

Like a classic epic,
she mystified my heart with her presence,

Then she smiled; a poetry paved its own way to reveal
my devotion towards her...!

Her silence echoed like verses unsaid,

Each glance of hers etched lines in my head,

She became the rhythm in every word I bled.

The Smile That Taught Me Poetry

With her teaching, she made her students into professionals,

Then I became a poet with her smile...

Her words planted seeds of courage in my mind,

Her presence turned ordinary moments into rhyme,

And her care carved strength in every line.

The Smile That Leaves Me Wordless

I felt so strange when teardrops
rolled down from my eyes

As I looked at her from a distance—

Without reason, like a season,

The inner feelings are unpredictable;

Sometimes they give pleasure,

and suddenly pull me into the deep pit of grief.

The love which is unexpressed

Is like an unused lute,

And it even frightens when overexpressed.

Many times when I try to say what I truly feel,

My tongue turns into my foe—

And flunks to give even a word.

That excitement, and that terrible feeling,

Together shake my heart with nervousness.

As my eyes yearn to see that desired face,
Happiness overflows,

And the smile—suffered through love—Gives an
inexplicable experience When I get to see her stand
before me.

That mystifying moment arrives,

And confuses me—whether to admire or to praise her,

For nothing in this world Could ever give such a feeling,
Except her.

Receiving what we expect is such a blessing—

And in this way, I'm the most blessed...

Because every time I look at her,

She offers that staggering smile.

Even the dictionary fails

To describe her beauty—

For it runs short of words!!

She, the Epic My Heart Chose to Read

A room full of books,
But all I read is her face...
She is the epic,
Who sat right in front of me.!
She sprinkled her smile,
And made my heart flutter,
Like a heavenly bird in paradise.
With her every move,
She made my memories sweet;
I hold her in thoughts,
To keep my mind neat,
And I love her,
With every beat of my heart…!

My Teacher-The masterpiece of God

Her face is the only beauty
That my eyes long to see often.
Her words are the only music
That my ears love to listen to—always.
Her thoughts are the only path
Where my mind loves to wander...
Her smile is the only thing
That holds my happiness together.
Her heart is the only place
Where I would love to be—forever.
And she's the masterpiece of God,
Whom my fingers love to write about.

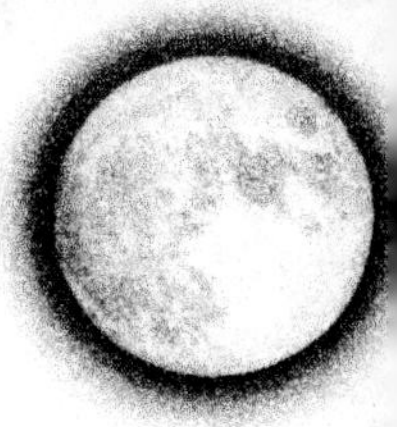

She is the one

Who changed my thoughts,

And shaped my life...

She is my Teacher—

And I also call her

My Guiding Star.

The Only One My Heart Thinks Of

The sparks that you've spread
Through your smile,
Filled my lonely soul with glowing happiness.
And within a glance,
You made a million stars wink together.
It needs no great effort to fall for you,
As you make everyone slip with your look—
And so am I.
A thousand times I fell,
For the way you react.
I love to love you madly,
As you're the only cure for all my aches.
It's hard to pass even a second,
Without your image in my eyes.
I let myself adore you without blinks,
For you're the only one my heart thinks...!

The One Who Took My Words

It's from her I learnt vocabularies;
But I wonder,
Why she plucks all my words
Every time I see her face...?
My tongue forgets what it knew so well,
My silence speaks louder than I could ever tell,
And my heart scribbles poems it dares not spell.

When You Cross My Mind

A sudden bliss,

While walking through the lane;

An instant smile,

That blooms from the lips

Without my knowledge.

Everything happens,

When my heart consciously holds your thoughts...!

A silent breeze hums your name,

The sky blushes in your shade,

And time forgets to move ahead...

The Way She Speaks

It's not a strange language she speaks—

A familiar one, in an unfamiliar way.

At the very first word,

My pale mind becomes enchanted.

Such flavourful words,

Spoken in an assorted, adorable tone,

More pleasant than melodies I've ever heard.

She draws everyone in—I swear.

And I? I'm not just attracted...

I've fallen—deeply,

Devoted entirely to her.

More Than a Heartbeat

I know that you're the one
Who controls my heartbeat;
And this time, when I miss you,
I found that you not just control—
But became my whole heart already...!
Now every silence echoes your name,
Every breath seeks your trace,
And every beat lives only for you.

Fathomless

My heart finds a way to tell you
What I feel,
But my lips suffer a lack of words
Each time I see you.
It's so easy to love you,
But the hardest of all is missing you.
I know how to be with you,
But never learned to survive without seeing you.
Miles mean nothing
When I think of the way you smile.
Is there any better way to survive
Than to hold you in thoughts and smile—
With no sense at all..?
My love for you grows...
Gradually, divinely, innocently.

And when I tried to measure it,

I found that...

It's fathomless.

If Not You, Then None!

Like a splash of water,
You entered my heart with no sign...!
By seeing your moonlit face and pure heart,
Poetry pours out from my fingers;
Love glides out of my eyes.
The ultimate surprise of my life—
Didn't you realize it's *you*?
You never fail to surprise me,
Each time with your soul-plucking smile...!
It's my only heart that suffers,
With a lack of words and skipped beats.
I lose my senses and all control
In your presence...
But my mind records your smile,
And never, ever fails
To rewind it—often.

My soul showers divine love,

Beyond control and beyond limit—

Only for you.

And it says…

If it's not for *you*,

Then it's for none.

In The Light of Your Smile...

You're my definition of love
And the description of beauty.
You never know the worth of your smile,
And I never know how to explain it.
But when you smile,
My heart blushes in an inexplicable way,
And my entire world blooms...!
Even the silence feels complete,
The stars seem closer than before,
And every moment turns into poetry.

Closer Than the Moon

Let me pull down the moon,

And make it closer to you!

Only then will you know

How my heart feels every time I see your face...

Like tides rising to a silent pull,

Drawn helplessly toward your light.

Even the stars pause in wonder,

Watching the grace, you carry so effortlessly.

No poem can match your presence,

No sky can mirror your glow.

You're the rare kind of beautiful

That even the moon would bow to...!

The Poetry in Her Voice

The way she talks about her past

Is a kind of delectation.

Even her pain holds a rhythm so soft,

It teaches my heart how to listen.

And the feeling she shares

Is something more poetic than sonnets...!

Her Smile-My Celebration!

The sunrise and moonlight
Can't move my mind;
The rainfall and thunder
Can't distract my heart.
The waves and breeze
Can't even touch my thoughts.
I never mind whatever happens,
My dear Teacher—
But when *you* smile,
It becomes my celebration...!

When Love Turns into Art

Meeting you is like painting a piece of art,
Because the hues of love
Splash around all my ways...!
You've inspired me in such a way
That, all of a sudden,
All my scribbles have turned into poetry.

A Glimpse of Heaven

Looking at your face
While you pray
Is an absolute bliss.
It feels more delectable
Than watching the dark night sky
Filled with infinite stars...!
There's a light in your stillness
That outshines every constellation.

Meta Dream

Can you hear me
Talking with you in dreams?
It's what makes me love sleeping—
But missing you becomes harder.
Dreams try to compensate for reality,
But when I see you in my sleep,
I start to regret reality
And crave only dreams.
Talking to you is already a dream,
And when you visit,
It becomes a *meta dream*!
And when you smile out,
Everything turns divinely magical...

22nd April

Every day brings a new hope

In everyone's life,

But this day—only *this* day—

Demonstrates Heaven to me

Every year...!

Because it gifted the world *You*,

And gifted *me* my reason to admire and grow.

Poetry in the Summer Sky

If skywriting were possible
By ordinaries like me,
I would've written your name above—
In letters woven with longing and light—
So even the winds would whisper you.
Then the clouds would've showered
With poetry, even in this summer...!

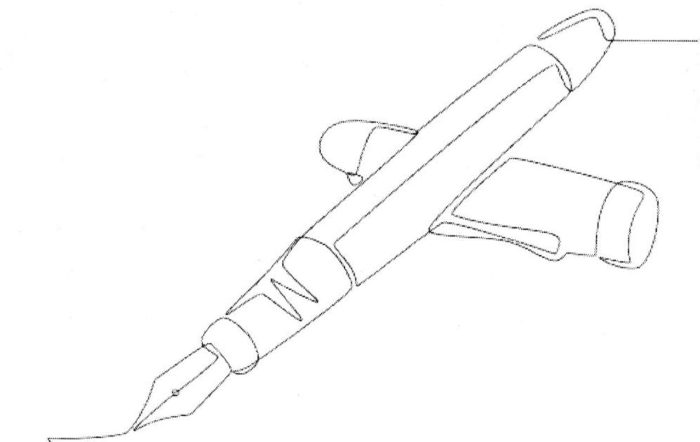

Quarantine: A Time I Missed You Most

What would I do
When the rain splatters?
It raises my yearning
To see you.
Whom will I tell to,
While all my thoughts
Are engrossed in you?
Rewinding the ways we conversed,
To lead my quarantine days—
As I feel cursed.
The only thing that pauses my scream,
Is your face
That comes in my dream.

Your memories visit me in queue,
As they are infinite—not just a few—
And paint me with an eternal hue.
How do I tell you
I'm missing you
Like a winter without dew?
Too many things
My eyes have to view,
But in everything,
I search for *you*...
May my heart and mind
Be encircled in you,
Until the moment arrives—
For me to meet you.

A Pattern of Poetry for My Miss

From blunders and thunders,

To ponder and wonder—

With blurs and errs,

By winking and thinking...

In image and words,

A mixture of sound and silence,

With flavours of butter and sugar,

Garnished with truths and lies.

A connection of bits and pits,

That alters swings and wings—

To reveal and heal,

Tied up with bond and fond.

Like a piece of touch and feel,

It makes one hiss and bliss...

This is the pattern I follow each time—

To form a poetry for **My Miss**.

Until You Return, Miss...

How cruel the passing of time is,
When there's no way
To see my desired face...
How do I confine
This pity little heart,
That often screams
To glance at that smile?
It's unusual to be apart
For this long a time—
I even curse nature
For what it's doing to me...
It has made my mind inutile,
And my hope fades
Gradually.

Is there any other way

To convince my inner soul?

The one that only laments

For the feel you once gave away...

An unidentified agony—

I'm unaware of how to deal with this.

And sleep is my only escape,

To expect you in a dream, as a surprise.

My pity little heart

Knows no other way,

Than to circulate your thoughts

All over my days...

She Feels Me from Afar

There is nothing more beautiful than this,
Being understood despite distance...
Like, whenever I think of Her from here,
She senses there...
A silent bond beyond time and miles,
That echoes through our unsaid smiles.
Even the wind seems to whisper her name—
Right when I miss her the most.

Everything Seems Right, But Miss Is Away

Everything seems perfect to me—
Cozy time at home,
Lone space with favourite melodies,
Some good books and hot coffee,
The weather,
And the memories it brings back...
Yes, everything feels perfect...
Except,
The thought of missing you,
And these days that pass
Without a single glance
At your face.

All Rhymes Lead to You

If Love is what we feel and deal,

Treat and bleat,

Breathe and wreath,

Learn and yearn,

Do and screw...

Then Love is absolutely **You**—

And it's undeniably true!

I find Love in everything that reminds **You**...

In dreams that stay and thoughts that play,

You echo in me every single day.

The Kind of Love Only I Hold for You

Not everyone who has a heart, has Love.

Not everyone expresses it the same way.

Not everyone who Loves,

Expects to be Loved in return.

Love's beauty lies in its uniqueness—

And certainly,

Not everyone who Loves You

Has the madness I hold for You...

Madness that purifies my whole being,

And elevates me

In every possible way.

With Her in My Heart, I Can Face It All

What an incandescent smile!
It splashed hues
All over my sky—
Just in a glimpse of that divine face.
Instantly, I retrieved my lost peace;
A moment I yearned for so long,
Now arriving—
Silently refining my whole being.
The words from my desired one levitated,
Like winter dew,
Showering over me in quiet imitation.
An echo of my name pervaded from your voice...
That's when I realized my purpose, my worth.
And by holding You
In my heart and thought—
I can face life,
Whatever may come my side.

The Ageless Glow of My Teacher

She's aging like the ageless Wine.
Gleaming in and out all the time.
What'd be gorgeous than her?
As she glows more each passing year.
Extremity surpasses in every simple move,
She indifferently inspires and leaves one with no clue.
Such a wondrous woman she is!
Her emotions-Like a bee in a flower, she conceals.
How to glorify the most charming creature?
Despite anything
she's dearly called
'The world's sweetest Teacher'...!

Where Dreams Begin with Her

You're in between my eyelids—
Standing over and smiling in such a way...
Even my eyes refuse to close,
So do I undergo lack of sleep.
Your glimpse lingers like moonlight in mist,
My dreams await where your thoughts exist.

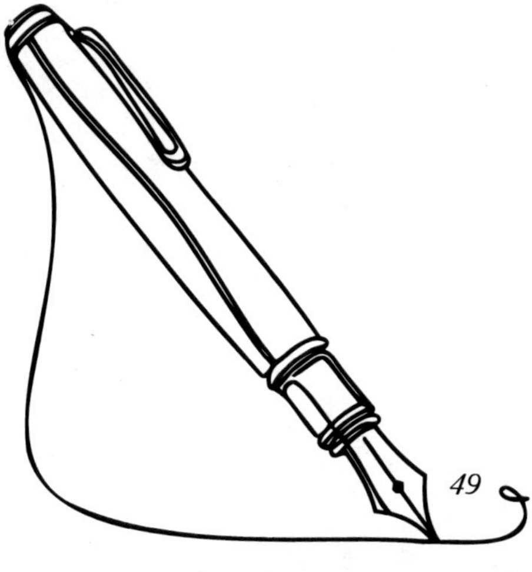

In Her Light, The World Makes Sense

I want everything in this cruel world
To be an illusion—
Except You, and that alluring smile,
That which helps me survive...
When chaos surrounds and lights grow dim,
Your presence glows like a sacred hymn.
In You, I find the world I wish to live in.

Unceasing: My Heart, My Love, You

Some regimens of the universe
cannot be ceased—
Like how the sun rises and sets,
The moon that shines,
The stars that sparkle,
The seasons that come and go;
They cannot be ceased,
By any means.
Despite everything,
The love I have for you—
It cannot be ceased,
So long as to you, my heart leads.

She Loves God, I Love Her

It's not about the way she looks!
Her beauty begins with the silence,
And continues to end up my sense in a smile.
In her not even a thing seems odd,
I love her more,
For her love for the God...!

The April-Born Angel

It's not about the day,
But the one who made it special this way—
The April-born angel!
Now I know why the sun shines bright,
Why it turned into summer, long ago that light.
You carry within you
The essences of the season—
Because you're the one who's chosen.
So temperate in look and view,
But it's spring that dwells in you.
You resemble the season's head at a glance!
The sun—lighting up the world of this universe.
And you—
Enlightening your students' world,
And their lives.

Where Your Hand Made Me Stand

In my school days…
Many things I've done and dusted,
But only you touched my heart—
And left it gently, beautifully rusted.
I never dreamt of becoming something;
Honestly, I thought I'd be nothing.
Then you came, all the way along,
Without even knowing,
You became my everything.
I used to wish for school days to end,
But it was you who made them pleasant again.
I have no words to describe you—
Just look at the moon,
And you'll see… it shines lesser than you.

You enlightened me,

You expanded my thoughts,

You patted me with your hand,

And just look now…

See where it helped me stand.

My dear Teacher—

I'm truly grateful…!!!

The One Who Takes Me to the Height

What a masterpiece you are!
How can one leave you without praising?
You revamp my spirit within a single glance.
I know not how
To drizzle the hues of love all over you...
Your name I whisper,
But my love for you is loud.
It rumbles, it booms, it swoops—
It batters me and pats me,
It takes me and remakes me,
It builds me, it senses me,
It soothes me, it commends me.
It helps me revive my soul,
And picks me up to face the world...

Every Art Imitates You

I find You in all the vibrant things
That depict Love,
Because I trust,
Every art that depicts love,
Imitates You...!
In brushstrokes soft and colours true,
In verses wrapped in morning dew,
In every frame, I'm led to You.

When She Smiles, I Shine

Nothing in this world could be the best proof
for my happiness,

Except the smile that shines on her face…

No sunrise could match the light it gives me,

No melody could calm me the way her voice does,

No prayer feels more complete than wishing
for her peace…!

When Everything Feels Wrong, She's Right

When I feel like everything in my life goes wrong,

Her divinely smile is the only reason,

That sets me to the path of flawlessness.

It heals what words never could,

And whispers hope, just like she always would...

Beautiful Is the Thought of You

Sleeping with your thoughts is beautiful,

But with the thought of your smile being awake is something delectating.

It blooms in the corners of my midnight mind,

Turns silence into a lullaby so kind,

And lingers like dawn before it touches the sky...

In All That I Am—I See You!

I see you,

When my heart feels overwhelmed with joy.

I see you,

When my mind feels empty.

I see you,

When I have none to talk with.

I see you,

When I feel depressed.

I see you,

When I want to share my feelings.

I see you,

When something troubles me from inside.

I see you,

When I get distracted.

I see you,

When I feel bewildered.

I see you,

Anitha Mgm

When I listen to melodies.

I see you,

When the wind blows.

I see you,

When rain falls.

I see you,

When the new moon shines.

I see you,

When I cross a beautiful place.

I see you,

When sadness kills me.

I see you,

When I walk a lone road.

I see you,

When I fall asleep.

I see you,

When I feel worthless.

I see you,

When I go sick.

I see you,

When I need guidance.

I see you,
When someone pokes me from behind.
I see you,
When the day starts and ends.
I see you,
Within my heart and eyes.
I see you,
In my fears and tears.
I see you,
In each of my smiles.
I see you,
Inside my heart and might.
I see you,
Like a worshiper sees the God.
I see you,
Not with my eyes—
But with all my soul,
And all my love...!

She Walks, She Smiles, I Write

The way she walks,

The way she looks,

The way she teaches,

The way she reacts,

The way she thinks,

The way she listens,

I admire her.

But then, she smiles...!

The stream of poetry flows with no cease...

Every word I write begins with her light,

And ends in the warmth of that smile so bright.

She Speaks Without Words

Even an expertised linguist can never learn,
The language of her heart...!
She never uses words to express
What her heart feels.
But in the silence between her glances,
In the stillness where her eyes pause,
A thousand unspoken verses unfold...
Her smile says it all...!

The Mansion of Self-Control

I know something about her,
Something I observed...
Her face glows when the wind blows,
She forgets her pain when it rains.
Not a talker, but an observer she is.
She never pokes her students,
But pats them with advice.
She loves art with all her heart.
An introvert she is,
But empathy dwells within her.
She holds on to her past—
Though she smiles,
I can see soberness deep in her eyes.
She never reveals her thoughts openly,
For self-control has built its mansion in her.

She's more sensitive than a flower;
Words spoken behind her back, hurt her.
She quietly supplies positive vibes
To those who truly know her.
She is an enigmatic woman,
Built with enormous goodness.

She, the Beautiful Art

She loves art,

Not knowing that

She herself is a beautiful art.!

I wish she could be aware

Of how much I think of her...

Making memories with others is an act—

And with her, it's not just an act,

But an art.!

She's the art that silently lives in my heart,

Every thought of her is a stroke set apart,

And her presence—an unseen yet eternal part...!

To Exist Around You

The mirror that you look at daily,

The tree that you cross every day,

The pen that you use to write,

The flower that decorates your hair—

I desire to be any one of these things,

Just to admire in the way they admire you...!

To exist in your world, even as a silence,

Would be more than a dream for my presence...

To Make Her Understand

Why am I in this world?

To do something extraordinary?

No, my mind replied.

Just to make her understand,

How worthy she is...!

The heart concluded.

Perhaps my purpose is not in grand deeds,

But in making her see the beauty she holds,

To show her that she's more than enough,

More than she could ever understand...

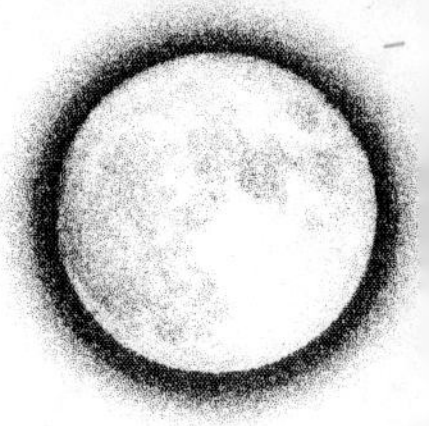

Your Smile Can Rain My World

You admire the beauty of rain,
Without realizing that
Your single smile can rain my world.
It's in you I find beauty—
The kind that can't be described
In words or voice.
Something inexplicably strikes my being,
Whenever I look at you.
You're extraordinarily beautiful in heart,
And so, on your face—it reflects.
I adore every little thing about you,
That turns my thoughts into dew...

She Outshines the Moon

Dear Moon!

You look divinely beautiful,

But not more than the one

Who I love...!

If sweetness is a woman,

Then she is the queen of it.

Even your glow borrows her grace,

She walks like poetry dressed in light,

And speaks like silence softened by love...

As She Travelled, The World Paused

The Sun and the Moon
Travel together—
With their only sparkling star.
The bus is no longer a bus,
But a wheeled cloud in motion.
The sky, though it feels an emptiness,
Still showers them with care.
The breezy air gazes through the window,
And gently admires the scene.
The night bird travels along,
Fluttering near to bid them goodbye...

The Poem I Admire

You're a poem—
With not just readers,
But infinite admirers;
And I'm one among them.
Devoted to your words,
Impressed by your tone,
Delectated through your imageries.
You're a poem with no end,
Where entire beauty is personified.
Your simple verses hold profound themes,
And mystify each one with their rhyme scheme.
You're a poem that brings delight,
Turning every darkness into daylight...

Not Just a Teacher

How come you taught me Love,
When teaching lessons is your duty?
Am I the only one
Who got devoted to you?
You play the role of a Goddess—
More than just a Teacher.
If all your students start to describe you,
They'll end up creating a beautiful art.
Have you ever wondered
About my love for you?
It's not an unconditional one,
But with only one condition—
To see your smile.
The stars are infinite,
And so is my love for you—
With no limit.
If you think my poems are meaningless...
Then let me create an epic on you.

Her Expressions-Beyond the Climatic Change

I observed her facial reaction for once,

And felt the beauty of climatic change is nothing,

Before her...!

The sky may shift its hues and winds may sing,

But none match the silence her expressions bring.

She smiles—and even the sun forgets to shine
its own light.

The Unseen Glance I Crave

The way she reacts

While reading my poetries;

The only moment I yearn to experience...!

To catch that slight curve on her lips,

To witness her eyes, pause on a line meant for her,

To silently admire—how she admires herself
without knowing...

Even God Knows…

When I try to write about You,
I often prefer God's help—
Because only He knows
How hard it is
To describe your inexplicable beauty...
Even metaphors fall short to match You,
Even the ink feels shy to sketch You,
And even my heart stays still—just to sense You.

The Smile I Breathe For

Your smile is my necessity;
Sometimes when you skip smiling,
I struggle breathing...
It's the sunlight my soul waits for,
The cure I silently seek each day,
The only reason my storms feel calm.

When I Miss Her...

If missing her is an ocean,
Then I'm a wrecked ship;
Fully drowned and half dead already...
Each wave whispers her name to me,
The salt in the air tastes like memory,
And the shore feels farther with every heartbeat.

Her Cotton Sarees and The Calm She Carries

I was never moved by any piece of Art before;

But seeing her wearing cotton saree,

Just stunned my mind,

And healed my heart...!

The folds spoke stories her silence held,

The breeze paused just to see her pass,

And I stood there-lost in the elegance
she carried with every step.

The Shortest Way to Paradise

If the earth has some ways
To reach paradise;
Then Your Smile is the shortest of all...!
It speaks to the soul without a sound,
Heals what even time can't mend,
And brings the heavens a little closer to the ground...

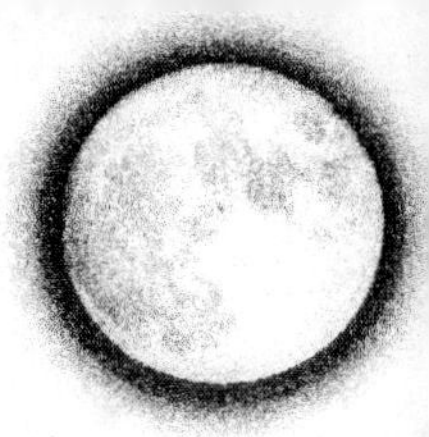

She, Who Holds My Light

She is a woman,

Who inspired me with infinite reasons.

She is a woman,

Who taught me what Love is.

She is a woman,

Who is behind my smile.

She is a woman,

Who showers me with Happiness.

She is a woman,

I love to write about.

She is a woman,

Whose smile changed my life.

She is a woman,

I yearn to talk with.

She is a woman,

Whose memories make my heart pump.

She is a woman,

Whom I think about—day and night.

She is a woman,

Whom I love with all my heart.

She is a woman,

Who became the Teacher of my Fate.

She is a woman,

Who holds no hate.

She is a woman,

Who lightened my Life's gate..!

The Heart That She Holds

It's not that she has everything in her hands;
But she gives everything my heart wants.
Because that's the place in me,
Where she stands...
Her love fills the voids I never knew,
With a touch so gentle, it feels like the dew,
And in her presence, my world feels new...

In Her, Beauty Finds Its Metaphor

She taught me what simile and metaphor means,
Without realizing that she herself
Is an actual metaphor of beauty...
Her presence a metaphor for peace,
Her smile, a simile of the sun's release,
In her, all the world's wonders find their place.

The Kindness That Keeps Me Awake

The world is sleeping, but not me.
My eyes are not tired,
But overwhelmed with your image,
I didn't lose sleep—
Just stayed awake with your thoughts.
Those moments when you laughed,
Wander endlessly in my mind.
You give me infinite goosebumps,
Simply by being kind.
And someone like you,
Is so rare to find...

The Essence of Her Stance

She is one of a kind,
Who has everything in her hands,
And the beauty of her soul is depicted
By the way she stands...
With every step, she leaves a mark,
Her presence lights even the darkest dark,
In her, I find both strength and spark...

Everything Changed, Just as She Said

Everything got changed,

As she told me—

She was right!

Everything shifted,

After I entered college life.

I started missing her,

More than I did before.

I started thinking of her,

More often than I did before.

My eyes began yearning for her face,

More than ever before.

She gave me more poetry,

Then she ever did before.

Yes, everything changed,

Once I stepped into college life.

She became even closer to my heart,
Than she was before.
I started loving her more,
More than I did before...

A Purpose Wrapped in Her Smile

The first time she smiled at me,

That's when I found the purpose of my life...

A moment so small, yet it moved the universe within me,

Her smile turned my silence into poetry,

And from that day, I started living—not just breathing.

The Day Grace Walked In

She was a stranger,
When I saw her for the very first time.
Heard her name from someone else,
She looked gorgeously simple—
A presence that felt warm and divine.
I kept gazing at her black and white saree,
Not knowing she had come
To colour my entire world.
She hadn't yet spoken a word,
But the way she stood, the way she looked—
Spoke volumes of who she truly is.
She doesn't smile often,
But when she does—
It's an incomparable beauty,
Soft enough to pause time.
I saw her move from a place,
And her walk—

More elegant than a deer's grace!

Then, she started to speak—

And a spark swept through the air,

As if a gentle voice whispered,

"Such a woman... she is your Miss."

When a girl fell sick that day,

She was the first to stay beside her—

That's when I realized:

Her character wasn't just made…

It was flawlessly created.

Like poetry that breathes love and care.

The Summer She Made Bloom

The hot sun never revealed it's summer,

But her cotton saree does…!

She walks like a breeze that cools the heat,

And summer feels like winter when I see her drape that saree neat.

If she places the rose, I gift, upon her hair—

That's when my spring begins to bloom, beyond compare…!

When She's Near, My World Pauses

I store all her actions in my Heart,
Because the mind never works When I'm near Her.
Her voice makes the chaos in me go calm,
Her presence erases even the loudest thoughts,
And when she walks by my world just stops...

She, My Living Prayer

Let me hold tight your guidance,
And your lighting words,
To lead my life on the right path.
Let me blindly follow your ways, like a devotee,
To enlighten my soul.
Let me learn from your character,
To shape my attitude better.
Let me never forget your teachings,
For they are my guiding stars.
Let me remember your little things,
For to me, they are everything.
Let me whisper your name always—
It's my chant of gratitude.
Let me speak about you each day,
Like a preacher sharing truth.

Let me love you like an aesthete,

For you're both my art and my heart.

Let me look at your picture with reverence—

Because I truly see God in You!

She – The Divine Co-Passenger

Yeah! I met *You*!

Not at school,

But in an unexpected, ordinary spot—

A moving train!

And just like that,

My train ride wasn't a ride anymore,

You made it celestial!

From afar,

A heavenly spark neared me;

It wasn't my eyes that saw you first—

It was my heart that felt you!

As I walked closer,

My heartbeat ran faster,

My hands trembled,

My steps wavered,

And my breath… skipped.

It was *You*!

I finally saw You again!

A divine gift to my vision—

It had been too long since I truly adored.

For the first time, I sat beside You.

I didn't know whether to live the moment,

Or just sit and admire You.

So, I did both, silently,

And thanked God—

Because only He could've made it happen.

You smiled... and I cherished.

The train was long,

But the moments with You were fleeting.

Then time tapped gently—

You stood, smiled, and waved goodbye.

You didn't just carry your bag,

But carried my heart with You,

And vanished in a blink...

Just left behind a thousand thoughts,

That now travel with me forever.

I Found God in You

What made me feel Your presence?
Was it the reflection of your moonlit face,
Or the spark of your divine smile?
What touched me so deeply?
Like a devotee who feels the presence of God,
I rejoiced within.
A devotee never sees the face of God,
But when I looked at yours,
I found my God in You...

My World Begins in You…

You're beauty personified,

You're Nature's delight,

You're the sun and moonlight,

You're a twinkling star and a raining cloud,

You're the whole sky and universe;

You're a bird's voice and a blooming tree,

You're the scent of a rose and the rose itself,

You're a surprise and a pleasure,

You're a miracle and a mystery,

You're an introvert and inexplicable,

You're April's light and December's night,

You're a poem and a painting,

You're an interesting story and a sculpture,

You're an epic and the epitome of Love,

You're pleasant and precious,

You're a garland and a guiding light,

You're simple and gorgeous,

You're God's masterpiece.

You're my way and destiny,

You're my thoughts and talks,

You're my dream and reality,

You're my words and actions,

You're my mentor and meaning,

You're my anything and everything,

You're my innate love and inspiration,

You're my happy place and peace,

You're my memory and motivation,

You're my favourite art,

And the only person in my heart...!

The Rain I Waited For

You're more than the Rain!
Rain just showers water drops;
But whenever You smile,
My heart completely gets wet
With Happiness...
No cloud can match the warmth you bring,
Even the drizzle pauses to listen you sing,
And every breeze carries your offering.

Anitha Mgm

Moonlight in a Moving Metro

Watching the moon in the night sky is usual,

But in the morning? Inside a train?

It was your glowing face,

Reflected on the windowpane.

I tried not to gaze,

But my eyes chose to stay.

Never before did I witness

Such a mystifying morning that way.

With the image of a divine smile,

I carried light in my heart all day.

It was you—

Who made me feel,

Who made me write this way…!

The Flowers That Envy Me

Those flowers on your hair—

They laugh at me, full of pride,

For resting on your head with grace.

Out of silent envy, I stare,

Their lasting freshness stuns me each time.

I wonder—

Do they make you more divine?

Or is it you who gives them their shine?

I go speechless...

Yet I feel luckier than those petals—

For I get to admire

The smile that lights your face,

A smile they never get to embrace.

Still, they seem proud,

Not knowing their fate—

To be tossed away once they fade.

But me?

Your thought alone endlessly waves,

Blooming in my heart,

Forever and always...

When Her Bangles Spoke

I was falsely inspired by many melodies before;
Until I heard the tone,
That your bangles composed...
Each chime echoed the rhythm of grace,
As if your soul spoke in soundless verse,
And my heart danced along, in a joy so immerse.

The Beauty That Surrounds Me

The freshness of a blooming garden,
The fragrance of blossoms so rare,
The sweetness of melodies in air,
The pleasure of a smooth, gentle breeze,
The waves of colours that put me at ease,
The joy of a sight so precious and bright,
The stream of poetry that flows with delight,
The divine power of being so true...
These are the things that surround me,
Whenever I see you, each day anew...!

God gave me You

Loving you is like worshipping God;

The action may vary but the feeling resembles...

It's God who brought you into my life;

To make a path, when I wandered in dark with no thought.

It's God who gave you such smile;

To make me treasure, when I knew no pleasure.

It's God who insisted me to see you;

To make me delight, when I had no light.

It's God who taught me how to admire you;

To make me write, when my mind had nothing right.

And it's you who completely altered me;

To enlighten my life, when I was in strife.

An Angel in the Form of a Teacher

It's You who introduced God to me!
I never ever felt His Presence,
Until I met You.
Are You an Angel sent by God?
I wonder because,
You're the one who protects me
From getting distracted.
If God had failed to bring you into my life,
How I would've been? I ask myself often...
You're a walking Marvel;
You bring Miracles,
In each of your student's life.

As usual You create Professionals, with your Teachings.

But brought a poet out of Me,

Just with your Smile!

It's beyond the ordinary.

You may not know everything,

But you know exactly what it takes

To light up your students' lives.

You're every student's dream Teacher!

Yes! Definitely,

you're an Angel sent by God,

Disguised as a Teacher...!

From Grammar to Heart: A Journey in Learning

I was unaware, When you taught me Grammar;

I had no idea, When you explained similes and metaphors;

I was uncertain, When you described the Themes;

I was unmoved, When you detailed the stanzas;

I got delighted, When you recited the poems;

I never learned how to apply them all,

Until I started writing about you...!

Only You!

Everything turned out magical
When I was with You.
No sense, no gravity—
But I was conscious of your smile;
That auspicious smile!
Words stumbled,
Time giggled,
And you mocked me.
A blissful moment, filled with laughter—
But it was Love
That merely mastered the scene.
No idioms can describe
The way you made me feel.

The conversation continued,

Topics varied,

But your smile remained still—

And that's my only will.

Happiness personified,

Joy overflowed—

Everything in your form.

I was overwhelmed and rejoiced,

And stood mesmerized.

It's You, always You!

In and around my self,

And there's nothing more

Than only You...

In Her Thoughts, I Breathe

To me,

Being alive means,

Being in her thoughts

And seeing her smile.

Feeling her presence in silence,

Breathing in the warmth of her name,

And feeling content just by looking at her face

You Smile, I Live

How unquenchable is the feeling
That I get from your smile!
There's nothing more worthy,
Nothing more fascinating to my eyes,
Than your smile.
Your smile—
Only for your smile,
My only heart yearns.
My delight?
It's only in your smile.
My pleasure?
It's the way you smile.
You make me smile,
Always—with your smile.
You just smile…
To activate my smile!

Prayer for My Teacher- The Creator of Professionals

Dear God,

In You, my Teacher finds her happiness;

And in her, I find mine.

When she smiles, I see You.

I need Your presence in every step I take,

So let my Teacher always smile.

She stands as one of Your finest creations,

In everything she touches, she shines.

She guides, she lifts, she inspires countless lives—

May my days be added to hers,

To create even more miracles in this world.

It's hard to take You for granted,

And just as hard to take my Teacher for granted.

You created everything in this world,

But she creates professionals

Out of ordinary people.

May her mind bloom like a winter garden,

And her heart overflow with joy.

May her inner strength grow beyond measure,

And may every desire she holds

Find its way to her.

Amen.

Catharsis In a Flower

The Glimpse of Catharsis; I undergo,

Whenever You receive the flower, I give...

Your touch, so gentle,

It whispers words my heart can’t say.

In your eyes, I see the warmth of day,

And in that moment, all my worries stray.

Anything for You

You made me an astrophile,
With your shining face,
And the sparkling smile upon it.
In You, I find my entire Universe,
Eternal sunshine and everlasting happiness.

When You look at me and smile,
Thousands of indescribable emotions
Walk through my mind.
In You, I see an image of love personified,
And the ecstasy of living life the right way.

It's easy for me
To ignore everything for You,
But the thought of ignoring You,
For even a second,
Will inevitably take my breath away.

There’s none my heart treats but You!

Anything for You, and everything is You.

It’s always You, and only You.

A Silent Affirmation

Because she smiles; I know she respects my efforts.
In her eyes, I see the reward of my toil,
A quiet affirmation, stronger than words.
Her smile is the light that fuels my soul.

She Runs in My Veins

My Heart pumps not with
Circulation of the Blood
But with circulation of Her memories.
Each beat echoes her name in silence,
And every pause whispers her smile.
Even in stillness, she keeps my soul alive.

Forever, Your Student

I came across hundreds of teachers throughout my life,
None was my favourite, and I was nobody's.
Then You entered,
Taught beyond lessons,
And made the word 'Teacher' more beautiful.

You became my favourite from the very first sight,
Undoubtedly, on every student's might.
I started respecting your profession,
Which made me see everything
From your vision.

When I wandered aimlessly,
You made me wonder about my future.
My goals are not my own,
But derived from You.

I never thought of being your dearest,
Just wanted to be the student
You'd wish to have.
I'm still indebted to You,
For You've shown me the right path.

No matter where life takes me,
Being your student
Will be the best reward of mine, ever

The Inspiration You Are

When I plan to surprise You,
It's myself who ends up surprised,
Each time by your smile.
Every ounce of my heart,
Showers so much love,
When You look at me.

You perform healing,
Without even realizing.
No conversation needed in your silence,
For your smile says it all.

If you smile and look away,
It means I caught your thoughts right.
The way you react to my unanswerable questions—
I'll keep gazing at you, constantly.

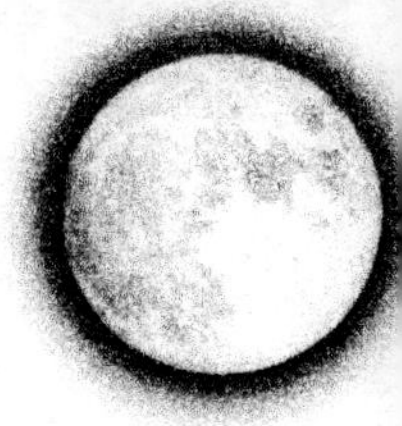

I admire each move of your actions,
And you inspire every inch of my being.
You're such a pure heart,
And worth a million pails of sacred souls.

The Heart That Loves Beyond

It's an addiction to see your face,
A good kind of addiction—
One that helps me grow, promotes joy,
And in which I find peace, endlessly.

Have you ever wondered,
How your smile changed my entire being?
It's in your smile I find my life's purpose.
It feels so delectating,
To hold you in my thoughts.

My heart!
It’s no longer mine,
It loves you a lot more than me.
My kind of love may be strange to you;
Just know this—
It will never let me down.

Placing you in all my actions,

Gains me more rewards;

And this reminds me—

I'll be nothing,

When there's no you in me.

To You, My Feet Walk

My days are not days,
Without seeing You in my ways.
I'm not myself,
Just loitering like a leaf that the wind sways.

I find no purpose to step forward,
It's always to You, my feet walk toward.
The yearning my eyes must see Your smile,
It'll change my state just in a while.

My days are not days,
Though the sun touches me
With its rays,
It’s all about You, my heart says.

The Surrendered Self

I'm no more a self-centred one!

All my self,

Already turned out to be You...

Every breath I take feels borrowed,

From the moments spent around You.

Even my silence now echoes You.

A Miraculous Fable

A portrait on my wall I drew—
The wall of my heart.
Well-painted with your thoughts,
And an image that resembled You.

It was just a painting,
No life, no sense…
Only until I saw You.
Like a miraculous fable—
You came!
You smiled…!

And the portrait was not just a portrait anymore.
It acquired life,
Started walking behind You,
And made your smile its soul—
As You gave it the will to live.

The Flawless Art of You

Your presence brings pleasure;
My heart whispers love
Every time my eyes meet You.

There's no better way
To understand God's existence
Than seeing You smile.

I light all my days
With your immovable thoughts,
And my life—
With the path You've shown.

All my goodness is not my own,
You're the one who's behind.
I'm no more a self-centred one,
Because all my self
Already turned out to be You.

I would gather the minds of your students
And the way they feel about You—
To make You feel honoured,
As those will be the most beautiful
And flawless art,
Without a doubt.

For the One My Heart Recites

I felt so strange when teardrops rolled down my eyes

as I looked at her from a distance —

without reason, like a season that changes with no warning.

These feelings are unpredictable;

sometimes they bring joy,

and sometimes they pull me into a deep pit of grief.

The love that remains unspoken

is like an unused lute —

silent and haunting.

Yet, when overexpressed, it frightens too.

Many times, when I try to express what I truly feel,
my tongue betrays me —
turns into my foe
and fails to shape even a single word.

That mix of excitement and fear
shakes my heart with nervousness.
As my eyes long for that familiar, beloved face,
happiness overflows.

The smile — though burdened by longing —
bears witness to a love so intense,
it becomes an inexplicable experience
when she stands before me.

In that mystifying moment,
I am left wondering —
should I admire her in silence,
or praise her aloud?
For no one else in this world
could evoke such feelings — only her.

To receive what we long for
is the purest blessing.
And in that way,
I am the most blessed —
— because every time I look at her,
she gifts me that staggering smile.

Even the dictionary fails
to describe her beauty —
for words are never enough.

The Poetry in Your Presence

I think that the Goddess of Poetry has
nothing to do with her power,
Because with your every move,
you’re giving me poetries,
whenever I hold you in my thoughts.
You turn silence into verses,
and glances into golden rhymes.

The Galaxy in Her Gaze

I found the galaxy in her eyes,
then she made stars in mine
with her sparkling smile...
The night bowed down to her silent grace,
as moonlight danced upon her face,
and time stood still to watch her shine.

Where Metaphors Fall Short

I loved the way she taught poetries,
But then her smile influenced me
to write on her...!
Every verse I ever knew dissolved in her presence,
For even metaphors seemed shy before her essence.
She became the poetry my pen longed to embrace.

Forever in Full Bloom

She is not just a flower to be smelt and left,
But a flowering tree that brings
happiness with its each blossom
Which is to be adored forever and ever...
Even the breeze seeks her scent in silence,
And the sun peeks through leaves to witness her grace.
She blooms not for the world,
but for the soul that truly sees.

Let My Name Rest in You

What shall I do…

When the moon fades into the sky,

And the longing to see your crescent face

Consumes my soul?

Every dream I weave is painted with you,

Yet my yearning never fades—why so?

Through the endless ticking of time,

I drift, lost in thoughts of you.

Where shall I go? Where shall I seek?

The bliss of your radiant smile...

Moments spent speaking with you

Linger as visions before my eyes,

Leaving no desire for anything else.

How shall I express?
Feelings too deep for words to hold...
Letters shape my longing,
Words carry my whispers,
And these verses, they are all for you.

Yes, I speak through poetry,
Until the day I see you again.
What more could I ask?
Let my name rest in some corner of you…

My Fairy Teacher

She knows my heart, she reads my mind,
In every moment, she stands so kind.
When joy erupts and I lose my way,
She calms me down with a gentle sway.

With just a pat, she brings me back,
Guiding me when I lose track.
Her patience glows, so strong, so bright,
A steady flame, a guiding light.

And when my world feels cold and blue,
She knows exactly what to do.
A word, a smile, a lesson deep,
She lifts me up when I start to weep.

She’s not just a teacher, she’s magic to me,
A fairy who sets my spirit free.
With wisdom, love, and a heart so true,
She makes my life feel bright and new.

Endless, Like You in Me

If my love jar filled up every time I thought of you,
dear teacher,

It would have turned into an endless ocean by now...

Each wave would echo your name so sweet,

Tides of memory pulling me in deep,

And in that sea, your light would forever glow.

Just Little Things

I never meant to cross a line,
Nor take your time as though it's mine.
It's just the little things you say,
That brighten up my dullest day.

A word, a thought, a simple cue,
Brings joy to me, more than you knew.
I never meant to be a weight,
Or steal your peace, or make you wait.

I now realize, I should have seen,
That silence, too, has space between.
You give so much, yet ask for none,
I should have known when to be done.

But still, I cherish every thread,

The little things you've done and said.

No more to bother, just to say,

Thank you, teacher, in every way…!

Epilogue

As these final pages settle, I find myself filled with quiet gratitude and overflowing emotion. This book is more than just a collection of poems — it is a piece of my soul, carefully stitched together with memories, reverence, and love.

First and foremost, I bow in humility and devotion to the Almighty — the unseen hand that guided my pen, gave voice to my silence, and blessed me with the strength to honour what my heart holds dearest.

To *her*, **Mrs. Merlin Geetha Sudhan**—

the remarkable woman

who inspired every word, every feeling, and every breath of this journey — thank you will never be enough.

You transformed my world without ever asking to, and I hope these pages reflect even a fraction of the light you gave me.

To her family, **Mr. Sudhan Raja and Mr. Ashley Raja** — thank you for sharing her with the world.

Her essence touched lives in ways she may never fully know, and I will remain forever grateful for your grace and support.

To my family, who stood beside me with unwavering belief, to my friends who encouraged my heart's voice, and to my dear colleagues who surrounded me with warmth and understanding — your presence is a blessing I will always treasure.

This book is for all of you.

With love,

Anitha MGM